FIELD HANDS

Mindful Stories from the Fields of Life

Pierre de Wet

**KE
PUBLISHING**

· *Words of Fortitude* ·

Copyright © 2016

FLUENCY

TELLING STORIES THAT MATTER

Fluency Organization, Inc. Design by Diane Kronmeyer.

Cover design by Kelly Doherty.

For Marnelle and Velmay

TABLE OF CONTENTS

Our Senses

FOREWORD

Publishing this compilation of Pierre's words in the same year that he left us is a spiritually guided work with grief and change as constant companions. I want to share just a glimpse of everyday life with a person who was a tireless champion of putting others first, a crafter of beautiful words (even in his second language) and, most important, a master of living in the moment. We spent years living in these moments and had "slowed down" to enjoy the fruits of Texas, putting days filled with passion projects ahead of more corporate endeavors. To Pierre, slowing down meant there was more meaning to the work, definitely not less work. His friend, author and entrepreneur Bob Buford, called it "halftime" in his books—the time in your life where contribution to society takes precedence. Pierre simply changed what his hands-on approach would focus on next. He transitioned from relentlessly traveling to the farms of America to his family and building a small local business based on being a mindful custodian of the land.

I transcribed his thoughts to paper for more than a decade of his life. It was an education I didn't know I needed. He brought an energetic balance of practical and impractical to the table each day. Like many entrepreneurs, he thought he should have a blog. Over a two-year period he challenged a little corner of the Internet with his thoughts about everyday life from a unique wine farming perspective. Both truly embedded in American culture and yet able to pull back and inspect daily life, Pierre spoke with a voice of positivity and strength in our politically correct world. We wrote a few posts to little acclaim, and it sometimes felt like a deafening silence on the other end of the conversation. Then we missed a week. We were "too busy." And the silence filled with people hungry for his words. They came to the wine farm for tours of the vineyards and asked about the blog posts; they emailed and they called. A special thank you goes out to all those angels who vocalized their love and genuine need for authenticity and kept us thinking out loud.

The creation of each short piece in this book was a beautiful volley of words between best friends, sometimes heated and then tamed to elicit the best story without compromising his point. The voice is truly his. Fragments and run-ons only help to emphasize his signature voice. Let me encourage you to take your time in reading these passages. Let them sink in. Stop. Think. And reflect on your own takeaways. He often talked about his dad, Dirk, a source of kindness and strength who could peel an apple in one long strand. Pierre's gift was the verbal ability to peel the apple of a story—one long thought carved without breaking. The nourishment many needed.

Pierre often referred to Kiepersol in his posts—the farm-based food and wine destination he began building in 1999 in East Texas. An elegant steakhouse, bed and breakfast, winery and distillery flank the beauty of a rolling vineyard. Here his vision was to grow artisan wines crafted to be comfortable to drink, pairing everyday life with the abundance of the earth.

A golden thread of nature runs through most of the posts in this book, as he was a man of the land all his life. He believed that we don't own anything in life; we are just caretakers. Farming was the best way he could provide that care for the land and for his family. But it ran deeper. I remember driving with him through an almond orchard in California. The neighboring orchard had cut off their trees at the base. They would next plow up the stumps and prepare for a new crop. While understanding the economics of crops and the necessity of the cycle, his reaction to the scene was as if he had been physically assaulted. The reality of the aging trees' demise struck a chord in his soul. Each tree, each animal and each person was a source of deep connection for him.

Soulful and dynamic in person, Pierre was a sounding board for a whole community. This same community has tried to console me by saying he was "larger than life." I know this life could not contain him. Still, it does not comfort. Pierre, thank you for the beauty you gave the world. I love you and miss you, and your energy still fills every moment for me and for many others.

I know we can only truly impact those who are ready to receive, but if we don't plant the seed, there is no chance for it to grow. So please share this book with others to plant the seed of mindful living at any age. Recognize yourself in some of the stories within. Grow those beautiful stories of your own and share the journey.

—Kelly Doherty

CHAPTER ONE
FREEDOM

WITH A GLIMMER IN THEIR EYES, THEY DREAMED OF TEXAS SKIES

And I will make of you a great nation, and I will bless you and make your name great, so that you will be a blessing. Genesis 12:2

MEMORIAL DAY IS HERE. As a foreign-born American, I especially say thanks to the thousands and thousands who bestowed on me the privilege of the opportunities and freedoms that only America can offer. Almost a hundred years ago, my grandfather left his military base in San Antonio to ship off to World War I. For many years his and their service were never correlated in my mind with President Reagan's "shining city on the hill" that we so preciously enjoy. When I think about the different wars, conflicts and various freedom endeavors, I can't help but just be thankful—without questioning the validity of each sacrifice made for our freedom. I believe in a military strong enough that nobody will ever dare to provoke the people protected by such a force. I believe everything is fair in guerilla and terror warfare. I believe in minimum force to stop them forever, but I don't believe in boxing gloves and face masks. I believe in nation building, if we do it here at home with the best-educated military force and the best-taken-care-of military families. We must give them the best opportunities when they return to civilian life after protecting every one of us—and those who cannot protect themselves—from evil and evildoers in the world.

We live in a transparent world today where hindsight says, "I knew it was coming." A transparent world where we have to be more firm and more deliberate than ever before to make it perfectly clear what will happen if you object to our freedoms, our God and our prosperity. I'm thankful to those we honor for their being so deliberate in the fight against tyrants, communists and socialists. And I hope and pray for leaders who can be wise enough to understand that unity brings forth strength, and strength will beware the foe. Our armed forces are and were our strength. I urge everyone to respect them, honor them and keep them in your prayers. And when someone cannot support them like we should, vote to get them out of office as soon as you can. Let's elect leaders who understand we are not everyone's freedom fighter, but we will fight for our freedom. I'm proud to be an American, and our kids and grandkids deserve the same pride.

A Camaraderie of Character

For no one can lay any foundation other than the one already laid, which is Jesus Christ. 1 Corinthians 3:11

THE DISCOVERY OF THE NEEDED INNER PEACE FOUND AT KIEPERSOL ... CAN YOU RELATE? From a sense of belonging, recognition, achievement and societal acceptance to a sudden desire for social privacy—when people realize they don't want to be labeled, and they don't want to be around the pretentious circumstances of everyday existence. An urge that cannot be contained to "just be yourself" develops, and you find yourself on an escape machine here, free from whatever it is you worked so hard to build.

Trapped within a tribe of expectation and performance, it's almost impossible to be free from the everlasting obligations. They are men and women seeking the finer things, people and places on a modern-day horse—exploring the hidden, still craving the exceptional. They escape here to embrace elements so fresh and deliberate, cleaning the air-conditioned staleness of their lives. An escape from the reins to the realities of true freedom. They find the freedom to broaden horizons, validate real friends and separate the wheat from the chaff (whatever drains the energy of souls). At Kiepersol, no drain—just green and positive vibes where everyone can be their all … on their own terms.

THE BIRTHPLACE OF GOOD

He said to them, "Go into all the world and preach the gospel to all creation." Mark 16:15

I T'S GOOD FRIDAY AFTERNOON AT KIEPERSOL ... WELL, I HOPE EVERYWHERE. A day that we call "good" because of the horrid happenings to our Savior. So we celebrate this day thinking about anguish, yet being excited about our own freedom. As always when I use the word *freedom*, I have to think about the unbelievable sacrifices made for freedom. Freedom to live in this wonderful country and freedom to know that our destiny is heaven and our many sins are paid for. I don't think I overthink things. But I think we're spoiled and not totally conscious when we squander these freedoms on a daily basis. We as mankind are unable to comply with 10 commandments, yet we have created thousands and thousands of laws wanting others to comply.

It is strange, the dichotomy of our society's inability to create a Good Friday and let the sun shine on all and let all be free and stay free without any strings attached. In what we call today's "modern days," we are consumed with things like desensitizing movies depicting barbaric times and are unable to spread good news, good vibes or positive recognition of what is good. The birthplace of good is small and innocent. The birthplace of good is illuminated by good news and kindness and care. So to each of you on this Easter weekend, we hope you can enjoy your time and the glorious good news with family and friends. God bless.

Raise Up Your Glasses Against Evil Forces

I am the vine; you are the branches. If you remain in me and I in you, you will bear much fruit; apart from me you can do nothing. John 15:5

THE VALENTINE FESTIVITIES ARE BEHIND US— ENGAGEMENTS, ANNIVERSARIES, SELFIES AND BEAUTIFUL WEATHER. Truly, memories were made here at the vineyard. The anticipation and hustle and bustle to make everybody comfortable in our world all worked out. And it was with the satisfaction of our farm lifestyle that we went to bed last night. It's always awesome to share our vineyard, our vines and our wine. Johnny Cash sang a country song about God putting something in a Sunday to make us feel alone, just us and Him. But I feel understood. I think God was a farmer at heart. Just thinking about the parable of the vine—the responsibilities and the labor with no fear for the things we cannot change. All I can say each day is, "Lord I hope this day is good."

Tomorrow starts a new week with new responsibilities, new rules and regulations and new people with the inability to manage and control their own lives. Bickering and attempting to make laws and rules to control our lives. What a fake satisfaction or shallow life it must be for your whole existence be a power play to control so many with your personal battles of inferiority. What's happening to freedom? What's happening to "live and let live"? If I think about the week ahead, I hope I can spend it in the vineyard and never turn on the news to look at the images of the same mindless few trying to control and coerce and put in bondage what God already set free. I hope your week is blessed and you won't have to be subject to the media—the wars that aren't ours and the pains we cannot kill. Live what is in your sphere. A lot of people over the years have said "forever," and sometimes it doesn't last that long. Enjoy it while it lasts. Be happy with yourself. It's an awesome consolation knowing that you're rare.

CHAPTER TWO
HAPPINESS

The Power of the Positive

Set your minds on things above, not on earthly things.
Colossians 3:2

O R SHALL WE ASK THE OLD ADAGE, "IS THE GLASS HALF
FULL OR HALF EMPTY?" A positive attitude might not
make things easier, but it definitely makes them more bearable.
More than that, it inspires those around you to embrace the
better side of the story. I get asked many days if the weather
in East Texas is good for grapes. As a believer, I believe that
all weather is in the hands of the Lord and he is good. But for
some people when it is hot, it is not good; when it is windy, it
is not good; when it is dry, it is not good; and when it is wet, it
is not good. That same weather attitude rules their lives.

We all have a cross to bear. It doesn't matter how heavy or light, or big or small, it is ours, and nobody else knows or understands. It's almost like a shadow that is with you wherever you go. But if you always look at the shadow, you will never see the sunshine that is always brighter and bigger than that little shadow you throw. We are so blessed, and there is so much brightness to enjoy that there is no reason to wallow. I see it time and time again that a visit to Kiepersol brightens perspectives and highlights blessings that so often are shadowed by place. By lifting the weak, you strengthen yourself and encourage the positive that makes life so much fun. And if you're positive and happy, you are part of us at Kiepersol. You are always welcome.

Absolutely No Reason to Be Miserable

Gracious words are a honeycomb, sweet to the soul and healing to the bones. Proverbs 16:24

WITH ALMOST DAILY, OR SHOULD I SAY NIGHTLY, THUNDERSTORMS BUILDING SQUALL LINES FROM WAY IN THE SOUTH TO THE GREAT PLAINS, WE KNOW THAT IT'S SPRING IN ITS FULL GLORY. We are close to the dry line where cold and warm atmospheres collide. The influx of Gulf moisture impacts big parts of the United States. But as much as some fear this weather and others cherish the rain, the warm and the cold contrasts will dwindle and summer will be upon us. A cool spring day like today can quickly turn into a muggy summer day before we know it. These fresh and clean days are made to be outside, made to be enjoyed, made for memories. I got to talk to a dear friend today. It makes me sad that he's so miserable in his rat race that he doesn't even realize there is sun and shade that need his presence as much as he needs them. Get out. Find a reason to be outside. If you don't have a place to be outside, we'd love to share with you. Drag somebody with you. Hold their hand and walk through the vineyard, or just sit outside and let the breeze clear your mind and the sun put life in the right light. I know we are blessed to feel it, live it and love it. And when I hear somebody so miserable with what life offers, I know and can prescribe the healing effects of the season at the place we call Kiepersol. Happiness is within your reach. Just grab it.

COLORS

I am the light of the world. Whoever follows me will never walk in darkness, but will have the light of life.
John 8:12

COLORS ARE LIKE TASTE. When tasting wine, most people without the requisite vocabulary will describe the flavors and tastes a little differently. Preconceived ideas and the anticipation of what something should taste like changes the experience, but all of that is not reality. So it is with colors. The color black has always been associated with success, prestige, notoriety, wealth, formality and fame. Why? Isn't this the color that makes us miserable? Everything that makes us feel the glass is half empty in our environment is dark. Dark clouds, dust storms, funerals and frozen crops all come with the darkness that we hate, but also subconsciously accept because it has been ingrained into our culture. Who knows why?

The things that make us happy are sunshine, bright skies, red and orange glows of sunrises and sunsets, clear waters, young brides with beautiful white dresses—the bright, the clear and the light things that truly reflect the taste and the flavor of the moment. When somebody is consumed with doom and gloom, we tell them to "lighten up." Get that heavy darkness off your soul.

We are living in a state of a confused delusion of emotions. But it's better days and happier moments just outside those closed curtains in the brightness of your ability to at least select the flavors, fragrances and light settings of your own life.

The Good, the Wonderful and the Ugly

Do you not know that your bodies are temples of the Holy Spirit, who is in you, whom you have received from God? You are not your own; you were bought at a price. Therefore honor God with your bodies.
1 Corinthians 6:19-20

HAPPINESS IS CONTAGIOUS. Walking into the tasting room the other day, I heard a young lady say, "This is the perfect pairing with wine." And her friend asked, "What is the perfect pairing?" She said, "This sandbox at the Kiepersol tasting room for the kids to be happy in." Kiepersol is a happy place. A place of kindness and service to ourselves and to others. A place where strangers become friends and where the experience turns into Texas pride. Where you want to be happy and you leave with a happy "wow." It's contagious. You almost want to make a list of all the special blessings that we all can take for granted.

At Kiepersol you don't encounter that miserable, self-centered, egotistical person who displays the lack of respect he has for himself by the way he treats people around him. I am astonished that one human can treat another human with verbal lashings so deeply hurtful as to mute bystanders who just listen in shock, unable to respond or defend common civility and kindness. I hear us Christians say our bodies are a temple. But I also know it is not what goes into that body; it is what comes out of it. I know we are so blessed that we don't encounter those kinds of people but maybe once in a lifetime. It makes me appreciate who we are, what we do and who we surround ourselves with so much more. I love people. I love wine lovers. I love vineyard people. I love people who enjoy the finer things in life and share it with their finer friends and family. That makes our world so special, and that's who we want to be around.

Our Senses

Take delight in the Lord, and he will give you the desires of your heart. Psalm 37:4

WHEN YOU SPEND A CONSIDERABLE AMOUNT OF TIME OBSERVING PEOPLE AT THE TASTING ROOM, YOU CAN'T HELP BUT REALIZE THAT EVERYONE HAS SENSORY ABILITIES. They try to align them with a benchmark, almost like a Munsell guide for smell and taste. Husbands and wives, girlfriends and boyfriends, friends and family find enormous joy and satisfaction identifying the flavors presented by the wine or spirit. It's almost the perfect game because it makes most people search deep into their experience archive for that speck of flavor that just triggered an immense realization of familiarity—either a pleasant or unpleasant sensory experience in the past.

No matter how inexperienced people think they are in the tasting room, they do have life experiences to draw upon. That familiarity blends into a new memory that everyone experiences in their own separate and joyous way and confirms the fact that wine is happiness. Not just the alcohol in the wine, but also the fragrances and flavors that evoke emotions and memories sometimes hidden deep or forgotten many years ago. Most of all, the interaction of good fellowship around a bottle of wine accentuates the flavors of the season and strengthens the solidarity that's so important to all mankind. Live well, love much, laugh often. It's easy to do with wine.

CHAPTER THREE
FARMING

Pruning with a Purpose

Do to others as you would have them do to you.
Luke 6:31

M Y DAD USED TO SAY IF YOU TALK ABOUT WHAT IS
"NORMAL" WEATHER, YOU ARE PROBABLY GOING TO
LIE. Last week's unbelievable March weather in the middle
of February has accelerated our timeline for pruning. We
normally prune with every possible hand from the farm,
winery and tasting room. But this year we had to get more
help and resorted to Gateway to Hope. These people might
be homeless and might have some issues, but they reaffirm
my belief that if you treat people like you want to be treated
and work side by side with them, they will reciprocate.

What a pleasant experience. Especially when you consider the biblical connotations of the vine, of pruning and removing dead and unwanted wood. Trust in a season to come, trust in a better day and believe that you can bear fruit with kindness and respect for all. If you ever need help on a short-term basis, don't hesitate to call the wonderful people at a place like Gateway to Hope and utilize those people who in some instances have written themselves off. You can help write them back in. It's all about being local. It feels good to support what is local—the local good, the local needy, the local producers and the local hard workers in every field. We are so blessed.

Fond Memories

Jesus Christ is the same yesterday and today and forever.
Hebrews 13:8

THIS AFTERNOON AT THE DISTILLERY TASTING ROOM A GUEST LOOKED AT ME AND SAID, "THIS FEELS LIKE COMING HOME. My grandma had guineas." "Yeah, really?" I asked. I told him he might be the fifth person who'd told me that in the last week. For those of you fortunate enough to grow up on a farm with guinea hens (or who knew somebody on a farm with these birds), you can awaken that nostalgia right here.

For about 15 years, Kiepersol has had a flock of 100-300 guineas roaming all the vineyards and some of the nearby houses in the neighborhood. Weird-looking birds. But for most people, they're a memory of a noisy guard animal and a happy familiarity. They are our pesticide. Ours are halfway domesticated, but they are really wild birds native to Africa.

The other reaction I get so often is, "My grandma made wine." Or, "My grandpa made wine." Followed by a long, wonderful story about how they picked the native grapes, berries and fruit and turned it into wine. Living here and working here we sometimes take that nostalgia for granted. I know my grandkids are going to say, "We had guineas ... we made wine." I'm ready to hear your guinea stories and your home winemaking stories. Share them with us. I should've started writing them down a long time ago but did not. So please help me.

THE FARMER'S ALMANAC

This year you will eat what grows by itself, and the second year what springs from that. But in the third year sow and reap, plant vineyards and eat their fruit.
2 Kings 19:29

I ALWAYS SAY WE GREW UP GREEN LONG BEFORE IT WAS FASHIONABLE. We were organic when that's all there was. We lived in sync with what we needed to live with—a respect for cost, a despise of waste and an inherent ability to share what would go to waste. We lived a life without radar and weather maps but with local markets, merchants, friends and family and the needy. There was nothing wrong with taking a knife and cutting off a dark spot on a tomato and eating the good part. We were sustaining farmers. Child labor was a family honor, and seasonal produce was part of the joy of that season and something to look forward to. The staples were potatoes, onions, sweet potatoes, corn and beans—things we could store in a dark barn or in a dry container without it perishing. The perishables were consumed, canned or shared before they rotted. And when they did rot, they became part of the animal feed—either going to the chicken pen or the hog house. Coffee grounds were worked into the garden.

We live in a time today where we are so consumed with parts per billion and obsessed with green and organic, shelf life and appearance, that we hardly take time to enjoy and appreciate the abundance of "all-season everything." It is locally available and affordable without breaking a sweat and truly is the safest food anywhere in the world. Pick up the *Farmer's Almanac*. Read it and try to comprehend what farmers contend with just from nature, seasons and moon cycles. Then look at the sensationalism from the Weather Channel and thank the good God for the precious choices that are available for your kitchen tonight.

Farmers First

*You will eat the fruit of your labor; blessings and
prosperity will be yours. Psalm 128:2*

O N THE FARM TOURS AND TASTINGS, WE ENJOY NEW
FACES THAT BECOME FRIENDS AND FOLLOWERS. The
vineyard and winery life is so enjoyable when you have
fun people around. While building the Kiepersol tribe, we
always discussed how we should give more than what we
expected to get. And then suddenly it happens. You get
more than you expect.

One day one of the bigger winery tour groups had a
young lady (a well-traveled, new implant to Texas and a
girl living the exciting life of our state capital). She had
been a little loud and a little vocal since she got there.
We left the distillery, walked through the vineyard and

everyone touched and felt the vines. She was loudly by herself looking underneath and over the vines when I asked if everyone was ready to go into the winery. I held the door open and everybody crowded in. When the last one was inside, I climbed up the first two steps of the catwalk to be able to see everyone and saw she had her hand in the air like she had a question.

I asked, "Do you have a question?"

She said, "No, but hallelujah! I found a real wine farm in Texas! You have vineyards and wine tanks here like a real winery." The rest of the tour group looked at her as if she had lost her mind.

I said, "Yes, we are farmers first."

She said, "No, you people don't understand. I never see vineyards and tanks at other wineries."

By size, we are still a very small winery. By volume, it takes plotting and planning to get all the fruit at the ripe time into the right tank to start the winemaking process for a season that in some cases that might last 33 months. I don't know how other people do their processes. As I told the young lady, everybody's business model looks a little different, and everybody's goal is a little different. But we're all in a Texas wine industry that wants to make Texans proud. Everybody's got something that they do a little better, or smarter or a little more profitably. All we want is proud people enjoying us, our product and our place as their own. Go and tell somebody that we can spoil them. Somebody who can experience the loud joy that she experienced when she exclaimed, "I found a wine farm!"

Yesterday true enthusiasts from all over the state and beyond filled the tasting room all day long again. Wonderful people who are so easy to make happier because they are already happy people at a happy place. The enthusiasm of the Kiepersol young crowd truly rubs off and gives you that feeling of "we are suddenly there." Years of toil can suddenly be enjoyed by the people who understand and truly appreciate. I thank everyone who has hung in there with us. We promise we'll continue to try to make your Kiepersol experience memorable in that special, happy way.

CHAPTER FOUR
SEASONS

WHERE THE MOON SHINES

Then Jonathan said to David, "Tomorrow is the New Moon feast. You will be missed, because your seat will be empty." 1 Samuel 20:18

EVERY SEASON COMES WITH GREAT NEW ANTICIPATION FOR SOME AND ANXIETY FOR OTHERS. Yesterday afternoon when the first real cold front of the season came in, I realized, "*That's* what a cold front should be like." When the temperature really changes and you really experience the change. As farmers and land builders, we live the seasons of the moon and the cycles it brings with a certain "certainty of uncertainty." We plan and we produce, mostly for those who never dared to look up and create a moon shadow. And once again we say "thank you, God" for another blessed season, a bountiful harvest and a growing season with its full moons and dark moons, dry days and wet days, cold fronts and heat waves.

The season was captured as the 2013 vintage. And for those who missed it bottled up inside, we will bottle it for you. As the full moons come and go, so do the years and so do we. Every season, full of hope for some and without advice for others, brings its own joys and pains. And when we say "hello," we better mean it because there is always going to be a goodbye. Some seasons are short, some are 62 years, and no two the same. We thank God for every season and take shelter in His wisdom of what is best for all.

It's Bedtime in the Vineyard

A little sleep, a little slumber, a little folding of the hands to rest. Proverbs 6:10

As farmers, we are so preoccupied with what we do and what we care for that it is almost with a shock that we realize most people don't live the seasons. Yesterday somebody asked, "Why are the leaves in the vineyard so yellow?" And all we could say was, "It's bedtime in the vineyard." It's getting to the end of the day in the season, and the vines have done their job. We as caregivers are proud of how the vineyards behaved and are thankful for the crop.

Nature's sequences and seasons are running their course. The daylight is quickly shrinking, and as the sun sets over the season, so do the sleepy eyes of the vineyard. Once chlorophyll-filled leaves have now given their all to the vine and have placed into storage all that they can for the season to come. It is truly a time to share because the weather is good with fog in the mornings and a pleasant breeze at night. What can be better than sipping the fruit of a past season while seeing a vineyard that has done its best? Come and share what we live—the restfulness and peace that our farmer's world offers.

A New Season Is Upon Us

For we live by faith, not by sight. 2 Corinthians 5:7

ALTHOUGH THE WINTER IS STILL COMING AND GOING AROUND HERE, IT HAS CREATED A NEW SET OF NORMS AND A NEW SET OF MEMORIES OF WHAT WINTER IS OR SHOULD BE IN A SOCIETY SATISFIED WITH AVERAGES. Was it a little above average or a little below average? No, it was just another winter. It cleaned, it cleansed and it damaged those areas we didn't protect and hurt the nose and ears at times. But a new season is upon us. In just a few weeks we'll see the first buds and renewed signs of hope and life. A season of new beginnings and old considerations. A season where we can start with new disciplines and new appreciations, or we can just average out and continue some of the bad and do a little good.

And to top it off, this will be an election year with promises, plans and news that tear down and vilify to the point where numbness takes over and we again are just satisfied with the average. The average that speaks of hope and prosperity without responsibility. The average that speaks hate of history without having been hurt or helped. Poverty is immortal, but without someone's success it is doomed.

But here on the farm, it is a new season. It is a clean season—all we are going to do is the best we can without dragging the old seasons, the good seasons and the future seasons with us. Only this season, day by day. Trying to do the best for all with what the day gives us. We hope everyone's season can be like the farmer's season with thanks and gratitude.

Sustainable Harmony

Live in harmony with one another. Romans 12:16

CAN YOU BELIEVE IT IS THE END OF JANUARY? So much happened so fast this month. We've got a whole new brigade in Austin. Our local senators Eltife and Nichols are invigorated and just as excited as us about putting Texas first. Our ag commissioner and friend Sid Miller is wasting no breath to make everybody realize that agriculture matters. Oil prices are down, but somehow our state always had the resilience to come back stronger and better every time this has happened. All three of our spirits made hay with the medals at the New York International Spirits Competition. Our new release wines just confirm the phenomenal path Kiepersol has been on … making Texans proud with so many world-class wines. Patience and persistence—the traits of the farmer—always make tomorrow a better day.

Good politicians, good farming practices and hard work are not enough, though. What we live by is sustainable harmony. A harmony between us and competitors and us and our wonderful patrons, believers and supporters. A sustainable harmony between regulators and our practices. A harmony between our practices and our environment. A harmony that accepts what the weather brings is good for us because God's in charge. A harmony of acceptance not to buy what we need but only those things that we cannot do without.

The coming four weeks will be pruning time. More than 60 acres of grapevines at Kiepersol will be shaped and tasked with a crop to bear this year. The dead wood will be removed, and the good spurs and the right buds will be deliberately selected for a better crop this year. When you have time, swing by and come see what we do. It's a magical time so well described by the parable of the vine. Although the vines are still resting, our labor starts. God bless.

Spring Is Here

You will be secure, because there is hope; you will look about you and take your rest in safety. Job 11:18

S PRING IS HERE. And that makes the next four weeks the most vulnerable time of the season. As soon as these buds leave the security of their enclosed dormant phase, they are truly vulnerable to cold weather and harsh winds. They are like our young ones when they leave the protective environment of home. All we can do is hope that we did everything we could and say a prayer.

THE SWALLOWS ARE BACK

The birds of the sky nest by the waters; they sing among the branches. Psalm 104:12

IT'S BEEN THREE DAYS SINCE WE'VE AWAKENED THE VINES ... AND THE VINEYARDS ARE NEWLY GREEN. It is phenomenal. It is an experience that I've had for many years. Every year about this time, if you stand still and listen, you can almost hear them grow. So fast, so beautiful and so perfect. In three days what will become clusters of grapes are already showing. On Saturday evening after we awakened the vines, the swallows showed up. In happy flight playing in the sky, looking for the spots where their Kiepersol babies are going to be born. Can't help but wonder, *Are they the same ones that are back? Are they the babies that grew up here the year before?* Can't help but wonder where they've been, what they've seen and what sense of security this Kiepersol land holds for them to return to year after year and make this the birthplace of the next generation.

The spring is beautiful, and this year the tulips brought colors with the flair of a glorious, bright season. Wisterias turned purple and dogwoods look snow white in the bright spring light. And suddenly azaleas that were just buds three days ago are in full bloom. It's a happy, blessed season. Go out ... come out ... just touch it, see it and smell it. I know everything is covered in pollen, but that also is a sign of fruitfulness and hope. Spring is beautiful and spring is young. And when I ponder what season I like most, it must be every one. Come see us, we'll share.

Thunderstorms

Do not fear anything except the Lord. Isaiah 8:13

I GREW UP WITHOUT TV, WITHOUT WEATHER REPORTS AND WITHOUT THE WARNINGS AND ALERTS THAT WE LIVE WITH TODAY. But I think maybe I grew up a little bit more aware of the weather. Grandma used to say thunder is the sound of God's goodness. Sometimes we could smell the rain before we could hear the thunder. Many nights I looked to the horizon and saw the faraway lightning strikes and counted. Someway, we thought we knew how far away the storm was by counting how long it took before the thunder rolled after the lightning strike. Somehow, when it was horizontal strikes, we knew it was a wild and crazy storm. And with those strikes that just went straight down to earth, we knew it was heavy rain. Somehow, thunder and lightning for me were always associated with blessings. Blessings, and personal messages to me.

Today the news stations and the weathermen have sensationalized and fear mongered us about the weather. Almost as if you have no common sense to get off the lake when weather is approaching and head homeward. As if you will have enough common sense to check the alert when they send it. Stormy weather always comes with an emotional warning and an awareness to huddle down—if you pay attention. Stand on the front porch or just look through the kitchen window as the weather emotions play out outside. Weather comes, and weather goes. And somehow when you take time to look, smell and appreciate it, you'll find the time to just *be* ... and enjoy.

A customer told me Sunday morning, "Everything at the B&B and restaurant was so perfect." I asked if the storm bothered them, and to my surprise she said, "That was the perfect blessing with the perfect atmosphere for a perfect evening and getaway." It made me happy to hear there are younger people who appreciate weather like I do. When accepting it as a blessing from God, everything feels renewed and cleansed, almost a celebration where heaven meets earth.

ALL WEATHER CONNECTS YOU TO THE LAND

For as he thinketh in his heart, so is he. Proverbs 23:7

WE ARE ALWAYS LOOKING FOR REASONS TO HAVE EXCUSES TO MISS OUT—MISS OUT ON A DAY'S WORK, A BIKE RIDE, A DAY IN THE GARDEN OR MEETING SOME WONDERFUL NEW FRIENDS AT THE VINEYARDS OF KIEPERSOL. And it is all justifiable because we are believers, and we all know that we shouldn't do things against our better judgment. So day after day we put certain things on hold for very appropriately getting a rain check.

But I believe in the power of touching, feeling and experiencing the blessings of nature. Sometimes you get hair blown in your face, get a little wet or have to put on an extra coat. And sometimes we get sun-scorched in order to have that time so desperately needed to be outside. The unbelievable control that the weatherman has over most people's lives is a typical risk aversion. The same aversion so commonly used by engineers to overdesign, just in case those parameters set by experience fall outside the bell curve. People plan, eat, sleep and drink by the words of the weatherman who sometimes gets lucky and gets it right. (However, warnings and watches do need to be considered seriously.)

Being on the farm my whole life, I've developed a deep respect for the love and the power of nature. But I've never seen a believer's following and the patient resolve so sincere as the believers of the weatherman. Live a little, risk a little, get wet. I've never seen anybody melt. Those words of fear and astonishment that the mouth utters can come true. So can the words of positive thinking and playful enjoyment of whatever nature deals. There's a stark difference between complainers and creators. Which one are you?

Soak Up Some Sun

The sun rises and the sun sets, and hurries back to where it rises. Ecclesiastes 1:5

SUMMER SOLSTICE—A BEAUTIFUL NAME FOR THE MOST SIGNIFICANT DAY IN A PLANT'S ANNUAL LIFE CYCLE. We dubbed it "first day of summer," but as the plant's clock ticks, it starts the awakening process the first day daylight increases. It exponentially increases until today. That's the time when the plant builds, produces and prepares for the crop. From today on, every day will again exponentially decrease daylight hours. It's the process of storing, maturing, getting ready for dormancy, getting ready to survive that upcoming winter.

A cycle that humans used to live by—from now until winter comes—is the time to stow away and get ready for those gray, cold days and nights when many days don't look different. New leaves will get old now; green fruit will get ripe. Roots will store nutrients, and the productive hours will decrease. But it is all good news. We're halfway to Christmas. It is going to be a long, beautiful day today—the longest one this year. With lots of opportunity to laugh, reflect and love.

A long day to say thanks for all the blessings. And if you slept half of it away, you will still have time to walk through the vineyard, toast with a glass of wine and know how blessed you are.

It's the longest day—make use of it. Text somebody and tell them you love them, or even better, pick up the phone and call them to share some joy. Soak up some sun—those rays bring positive vibes. And lastly, most important, glorify the Maker of this beautiful day.

CHAPTER FIVE
CELEBRATIONS

Thanksgiving

Enter his gates with thanksgiving and his courts with
praise; give thanks to him and praise his name.
Psalm 100:4

DEATH IS A BIRTHRIGHT. Bought by blood for an
everlasting rest in peace. A right for running a race as
hard as we deemed necessary. A race to be kind to others and
one where we take second place. Death brings the transfer
of duties, obligations and true perspective when the reins
get turned over to the ones who can pick them up. It does
not discriminate except by age. This was one of those weeks
where the angel brigade definitely increased, and we know
their faces and their hearts.

Around this time of year, the winter starts showing
its beautiful white colors. So clean, so pure as our

thankfulness. This is a time of acknowledgment of the "so many things" we are thankful for. Let me start by being thankful for a Jesus who is so good. A country that still has promises. A state that I call my country. A wine farm that produces. And a family who can stand together through the happiest times and the hardest work, through pains and pleasures, while protecting and loving like only family can.

We are also thankful for a Kiepersol tribe we love and try to please with kindness and quality of product and service. We're thankful they come back again and again and that they spread the word about a place where they can forget themselves and live in the moment.

We are also thankful we can knock and doors do open. We are thankful we can ask and wisdom does come. We are thankful we have no one to forgive but we can ask forgiveness. We're thankful we can trust that the road ahead will be bearable because we are not alone. We are thankful we don't get what we deserve, but instead get so much more. We thank you for reading our thank you note to you and for sharing this thankful time.

The Christmas Lights Are On. Do You Have Your Permit?

I urge you, brothers and sisters, to watch out for those who cause divisions and put obstacles in your way that are contrary to the teaching you have learned. Keep away from them. Romans 16:17

It's Christmas season again. It's almost as if it's the season for the young'uns and the old. The older I get, the more nostalgic this season becomes. I remember when it was a time where I wanted to get things done and nobody worked. I remember how my irritation with dragging out the season made some call me Scrooge. But with peace and happiness, the Christmas season has again become one of my favorite times of the year. I love the Christmas music. Much of it I've heard all my life and don't get tired of hearing. Pretty soon the shortest day will be upon us, and by Christmas the daylight will already be increasing. At sunset tonight I couldn't help but reflect on the happenings of the year. We know that we are so blessed and so grounded by the grace of our heavenly Father through Jesus. But in all these blessings, we can't help but let our minds dwell on the recent weeks' news of racial discontentment, police brutality, immigration battles and so much more. And when I ponder it all, I believe the problem is with government.

We've become a nation of 300 million people living under a government that is succeeding in letting the sun shine on no one. For the life of me, I cannot think of a government agency that is there to help me, or you or anyone I know. We are a nation in fear of our government. Sit and think for a second and let me know which government agency you like to get correspondence from. I'm not talking about your well-earned social security check or your overpayment in taxes. Our government treats us not like "we the people" but like "we the lawbreakers." This same government has slowed down progress to a speed that diminishes any hope for a return on investment. They make everybody you hire a liability and everything you do monitored and controlled by multiple agencies. They even have a tax, a bond and a permit attached to every one of your actions.

It's not that there is discord between people. There is discord between people and government. No agency is there to unify the people ... in anything. I consider everybody I've ever met just good people who can make mistakes, but they are not malicious. Maybe I'm naïve or live in paradise here in East Texas. As sad as it is to say, I don't know of one law that makes it easier to compete, easier to make jobs or easier to live the American dream by enforcing our capitalistic Republic. I've never seen a language that is so clear but so convoluted for those trying to interpret our Constitutional rights.

I don't think we have a black and white or purple problem. I think our government wants us to have one; and at the end of the day when the sun shines on no one, when the people don't know the truth, they blame each other. Even those in government live in fear of government. What a vicious cycle. Fortunately we can still hug a loved one, for now eat a steak, drink an adult beverage and love our place and families. But try to think of the amount of regulations involved in just those few basics.

O Holy Night

*Therefore encourage one another and build each other up,
just as in fact you are doing. 1 Thessalonians 5:11*

I T'S THE SEASON OF ALL SEASONS, AND IN THIS
HEMISPHERE IT IS THE SEASON OF REST AND DORMANCY.
Three days ago was the shortest day and the longest night. It
is the season of our Savior, a time to celebrate a birth that
gave life and hope, peace and joy. It is a season to look back
and reflect, and look forward and dream. It is truly a season
of kindness and hope. It is a season when we're glad we don't
get what we deserve. A season when we learn not to run *from*
things, but toward the things we love and want. It is a season
of accounting and accountability. A season of counting losses
and profits. Losses of loved ones and losses of opportunities
to express a kind thought or a positive word. Missed

opportunities to be happy and filled with laughter, to spread joy and touch somebody with a hand of encouragement or a hug of understanding.

And in doing so, we start anew—resolutions, plans, dreams and goals solidified with prayers and promises. Start small. Start with the things you can touch, reach and handle. Start with the ones you can hug and hold. Start with yourself. Excuse the negatives; invite the positives. Say it with your heart, and speak it with your mouth. The biggest gift is kindness, and kindness grows kindness. Don't be boastful; we are all made in the same image. Be tolerant and forgiving because we will need the same.

I recently stumbled across a video of a beautiful seven-year-old little girl singing a song and was amazed by the amount of people who viewed this video. I normally don't look at ratings, likes and dislikes. But for the life of me, when I saw 78,000 likes and 3,000 dislikes, I had to wonder what kind of human being is so insecure that they have to dislike what a seven-year-old sings. Why can't they just say nothing if they can't say something good? Be kind, be gentle. God blessed us with this Christmas season and promised prosperity in Him.

Holding on to
Good Friday

But he was pierced for our transgressions, he was crushed
for our iniquities; the punishment that brought us peace
was upon him, and by his wounds we are healed.
Isaiah 53:5

IT IS ALMOST SHOCKING TO SOME PEOPLE THAT THERE
ARE STILL PEOPLE AND ORGANIZATIONS THAT HOLD
CERTAIN THINGS DEAR. Good Friday is the day we celebrate
the ultimate sacrifice for our eternal well being. It's amazing
how little value special days like this hold for so many
people. I grew up with this day as a sacred day, and as long
as I'm around, we'll honor it as a sacred day. In my feeble
calculation our souls were saved on a cross at Golgotha 1,981

years ago. Do I know that is exactly the right day? No. But that's the day we celebrate that love for us. So, we are closed on Friday everywhere we do business.

A Mother's Day Prayer from the Vineyards

Dear children, let us not love with words or speech but with actions and in truth. 1 John 3:18

WE SAY THANK YOU, LORD, WITH LOTS OF WISHES. We wish that every child will outlive their mother. And that every child has a mother who loves and adores them and makes them the center of their existence. We thank you for helping mothers to choose fathers who stay by their side. Lord, we pray that we can trade love for the life they gave us, hold them dear and near, respect them and have them respect us.

Help us bring joy to their hearts because we are delighted in the decisions they made to bring us into this world. Give us the opportunity to be kind and good. The opportunity to be an in-touch, contributing member of your creation. We thank you, Lord, for those who take the duties of mothers with so much love for those they didn't even bear. Lord, we love you. We love our mothers. And we hope that the fruit of our vines will produce the same love and admiration for future generations. Bless us to our mothers, and bless our mothers this day and every day. Amen.

FATHER'S DAY

Start children off on the way they should go, and even
when they are old they will not turn from it.
Proverbs 22:6

O N A FATHER'S DAY MORNING IT IS MIND-BOGGLING THAT I'M SO FORTUNATE. Every day of my adult life I have been treated like it is Father's Day with a "good morning" phone call or a "good night" phone call. An "I love you" text, or one asking, "Where are you, Daddy? What are you doing?" I have boxes full of letters from my father. We were just fortunate to love and communicate each day as if it were the best day and maybe the last day. When he passed away, I had no built up "thank yous" or "I forgot to tell you" emotions.

Today, Father's Day for me is just a day of reflection on how fortunate we are. But when you reflect, you also think of those less fortunate. Those who lost fathers and feel a void. Today I especially think of those soldier fathers—so many buried in so many places all over this country and the world. But luckily, I believe in angels. And I believe that someway, somehow they also were there in some guardianship, looking over us and looking over their loved ones. Guiding and protecting with the same love they instilled into the family sphere while they were there. Love is a happy sacrifice with blind acceptance of happy moments and not so happy moments.

Love doesn't forget, neither does it remember.

Love is positive and consistent, like that of our Maker. But there is no reason to have a void in your life, because the heavenly Father, the good Father, is more consistent and more reliable and more clear than any of our earthly fathers can be. Make every day a Father's Day, and this proclaimed day will become just another day of counting blessings and making resolutions to be there, not just for your own, but for everyone in need.

HAPPY 238ᵀᴴ BIRTHDAY

I will establish my covenant as an everlasting covenant between me and you and your descendants after you for the generations to come, to be your God and the God of your descendants after you. Genesis 17:7

THIRTEEN GENERATIONS OF AMERICA—WHO CAN REMEMBER, AND WHAT IS STILL THE SAME? Thirteen generations have fought, worked hard, developed, innovated, crisscrossed the country, built cities and dreams and raised families. Thirteen generations enjoyed the freedoms of the greatest place on earth. Thirteen generations made sacrifices—so many so young died for the freedoms that we so often take for granted. America, the champion of the world. The beacon of light and the envy of everyone. Thirteen generations who lived the Constitution written by men who verified that which was endowed by God. Thirteen generations who didn't always agree but who knew the Constitution kept us free. Thirteen generations who always left this a better place. When times were at their darkest, a brighter light showed up. A spirit of unity always prevailed. And that's what we celebrate—a country's birthdate as an annual reminder of who we are and how blessed one nation under God can be.

The nostalgia of generations gone by, the wisdom of great leaders and philosophers, the spirit of pioneers and firsts, men walking on the moon who planted a flag—all gave us a right to forever brag. We set the world free from tyranny with generation 10, our bravest men. Those big trees, now old and many gone, left us with an obligation to know that in unity we are strong. It is time to be proud and be Americans again with pride in our own abilities and resolve. Just look at our blessings and surely you would know that nowhere on earth are people so free— free to follow their dreams and live their lives and teach the next generations to still be free.

It's time to be authentic again. Buy American, eat American, drink American. Let your freedoms not be others' bondage. And let their freedoms not be your envy.

A QUICK
THANKSGIVING THANK
YOU

The Lord has done it this very day; let us rejoice today and be glad. Psalm 118:24

IT'S THANKSGIVING TIME AGAIN. As we get older we realize that every day is Thanksgiving, and we truly give thanks for each one of them. When you start making a list, you realize how blessed you are because there are so many things we give thanks for every day … especially this week. But our main thanks is to our Jesus. He's the reason we can say thanks and the reason that each one of you is in our lives and on our paths. Thanks to our families, our crops, our businesses, our friends and employees, our acquaintances, our wonderful customers and this year a special thanks to those who are "quickly." It feels as if the days are so short and the months and years fly by so fast that we really appreciate those who are "quickly"—quickly moving on the road, quickly returning calls, quickly responding with a happy face—all glad to be part of all the wonderful blessings. So we just want to quickly say thank you from Kiepersol. Have a safe and happy holiday.

No Pressure Christmas

Trust in the Lord with all your heart and lean not on your own understanding. Proverbs 3:5

I'VE BEEN KNOWN AS THE GRINCH. But I'm really not. I'm so enthralled with the seasons. Being a farmer all my life, one season is followed by another season and another to make a growing cycle. Here in the Northern Hemisphere, the Christmas season is just like everywhere else—a season of hope and thanks, a season of festive challenges, a season of an innocent baby born to suffer so dearly to set us free. Yes, the season of new beginnings. But the 22nd of December, what we call the first day of winter, is truly the beginning of the new season because every day from then on the daylight will increase. We'll see new awakenings, spring will come and fruit will be born. Before we know it, it will be summer with the fruit of our labor.

I started off by saying I'm not the Grinch, but I think one of the Grinchy effects is our inclination to set goals. The year-end is normally the time for the goals, and many feel they will be all right if they can just get through December, as Merle Haggard once sang. But if we can stand back for a second and not put that pressure of goals and timelines on ourselves, the chance for success stays the same, and the chance for disappointment disappears. Enjoy the process of going toward a goal. But don't set goals. You are not in control of enough. Patience and diligence is the recipe for success. And those who enjoy the process are successful. May God bless all of us, and may we be what He wants us to be. He made a huge offering for you and for me. Merry Christmas and a Happy New Year.

Fifteen Years of
Consistency

*We always thank God for all of you and continually
mention you in our prayers. 1 Thessalonians 1:2*

Today is the 15th anniversary of the Kiepersol
B&B and Restaurant. The time passes so fast it is
unbelievable. Some of the kitchen staff who started with us
are still here 15 years later. For many young men and women,
it has been the path to their ultimate goal. Valets turned
into pilots, bartenders into doctors and coaches. Servers
became lawyers, politicians, teachers, homemakers, marketing
managers and also self-made entrepreneurs. All the years
were good years, each with its own struggles, heartaches and

pains. In the years after 9/11 I had to say, "Better days will come" … and they did.

But most of all, today I remember our dedicated customers—the Kiepersol tribe—those in Texas who wanted better. Who wanted a place where they wouldn't be embarrassed to bring guests or family. Those patrons who understood that everybody just did their best every day. Couples who were among the first to have their weddings here now have boys and girls who are 12, 13 and 14 years old. We still get the annual returns to the honeymoon suite, and we know that good people made good memories. I can sit and reminisce over the wonderful customers who have passed on. Those who had their last birthday meal here because they loved it so much.

And then I can't help but think about those who showed up and said, "I can get a steak in town for $9.95." No, we didn't please everyone, but it was not due to a lack of effort. Our return customers—our 15-year customers— have been those unentitled people who appreciate and deserve something better in life, who work and search until they find it. Fifteen years of the same menu. Fifteen years of the best wines and plenty of top shelf to choose from. We never tried to mimic someone else. We always just tried our best to be the best we can be.

There are too many people to thank … even those who understood when a brand-new truck tire was damaged by a valet. I remember the joy on the face of an elderly woman when she said, "This lobster bisque is the best I've ever had, and I'm from lobster country." There's plenty of good to remember, and then there's also the customer who is back every week but we can never please—just trying to get something for free. It takes all sorts to make life go around.

Kiepersol is finally mature. It's finally the destination that we farmers dreamed of. We finally have a tribe of supporters who appreciate, understand and spread the word about a special place like no other. A special place where we cannot make unhappy people happy but one where real people can experience the products, pleasures and people of our farming lifestyle. They can immerse themselves, they can be a part of it and they can be proud of it. I thank every one of you and am looking forward to many more years of good memory making at Kiepersol.

FIELD HANDS Mindful Stories from the Fields of Life

Top 10 Review of 2014 Kiepersol Happenings

But those who hope in the Lord will renew their strength. They will soar on wings like eagles; they will run and not grow weary, they will walk and not be faint.
Isaiah 40:31

10. Built a giant (and I mean giant) sandbox next to the winery so the kids can have fun too.
9. *Sommelier Journal* features our Texas Syrah at 86 points.

8. Released a Studio 333-produced CD of Americana music to accompany my first book *The Story of We*.
7. *The Dallas Morning News* features the Kiepersol Cab in their "10 Outstanding Texas Wines That Are a Good Value."
6. Opened the Stable House to the public to be able to offer B&B rooms directly on the vineyard.
5. Kiepersol's Harvest Festival is transformed into the Kiepersol Vine Day—a casual gathering where the vines are put to sleep for the season. Look for the "wake up" in the spring.
4. KE Merlot and Barrel 33 win double gold at the Houston Rodeo Uncorked.
3. Opened a distillery next door to the winery.
2. Released Dirk's Vodka, Pierre's Rum and Jimmy's Bourbon (and Kaizer de Wet).
1. Won three awards for our spirits at the New York International Spirits Competition: silver for Pierre's Rum and bronzes for Jimmy's Bourbon and Dirk's Vodka.

Whew! It's been a fast-paced wonderful year, and there's much in store for next year. Thanks for being such an important part of Kiepersol.

Reflections on the Finer Pleasures in Life

Gentleness and self-control. Against such things there is no law. Galatians 5:23

WHEN FRIENDS AND FAMILY AND A LOT OF SPECIAL PEOPLE GET TOGETHER FOR AN EVENT LIKE THE PREMIERE OF DIRK'S VODKA AT THE DISTILLERY AT KIEPERSOL, IT AMAZES ME HOW MANY PEOPLE GO OUT OF THEIR WAY TO BE SUPPORTIVE, KIND AND EXCITED. You spend so little time with so many that you wonder if they know how much you appreciate them. But within the spirit of that commitment from so many is a herd happiness and the security of knowing we're not alone. It's having friendships and relationships built on mutual trust and appreciation for the good in life, and the good is always pure, honest and unafraid—unguarded and free.

My hope and prayer is that the direction we are going will stay pure and that the products won't be abused. That they will forge friendships. That those who use them will understand that the obligation of moderation, along with respect for themselves and for those around them, lies squarely on their hearts. My hope is that the products will never be misused. They are meant to be some of those finer pleasures in life that you respect and enjoy with caution because they can make you act like a fool and lose respect. We are proud of Dirk's Vodka, and we are thankful for so many who showed support—even if it wasn't for the product but support for *us*.

CHAPTER SIX
PEOPLE

IT'S A BEAUTIFUL NOISE AT KIEPERSOL

He will yet fill your mouth with laughter and your lips with shouts of joy. Job 8:21

ANOTHER WEEKEND HAS COME AND GONE. A weekend when I spent most of the time on the sideline ready to jump in and help wherever I can. In observing the next generation of the Kiepersol family, I hear them sharing their love and passion for their lifestyle on this Texas wine farm. I hear about a lifestyle without a beginning or an end. With growing seasons so different from the ones before and the ones ahead. I hear about better end results, better wines and better spirits every season. I hear them talk about the details—the details that I remember telling them are so important.

During the tours and tastings I hear another beautiful noise—the noise of happy contentment among proud customers, patrons and loyalists. Of people who keep bringing friends and family to experience the product and the place that we call work and home. As I close my eyes and listen to the happy noises and laughter, it makes me wonder: are only happy people coming here, or does this place make people happy?

At the restaurant amid the hustle and bustle in the kitchen, you can hear that beautiful noise coming from the dining room. A festive noise of people happy with place and product. Warm and sunny days always enhance the happiness. But I know that this place is healing to the soul because you can feel so close to God just listening to that beautiful noise. Have you heard it?

THE FARM & VINEYARD LIFESTYLE

Do not conform to the pattern of this world, but be transformed by the renewing of your mind. Then you will be able to test and approve what God's will is—his good, pleasing and perfect will. Romans 12:2

L IFE HERE ON THE FARM AND IN THE VINEYARD USED TO BE A LOT SIMPLER, OR MAYBE IT WAS JUST ME. Kids didn't *compete* before they *comprehended*. They learned by living the way we made our livelihood. They imitated and improvised. They worked alongside of me, not for money but for the experience of togetherness. They knew I loved them and would never hurt them. They knew I would always protect them to the best of my ability. And they knew I've always loved them for exactly who they are and not who I wanted them to be.

Something happened. Somehow that is not good enough anymore. I look around and see parents striving to "head start" their kids. Parents' own unfulfilled dreams of becoming pitchers, ballerinas, soccer stars, Olympic medalists or scholarship winners have manifested into constant compromises where kids and parents live lives of anguish and confusion. What happened to just being happy with productive, imaginative kids with good manners and morals? Has childhood been replaced with extracurricular activities? Is anyone happy with that rat race, and why would we throw our kids into it so early? I understand that the times and expectations have changed, but I also understand that a kid's ability to imagine, help and imitate in the shelter of a parent's shadow developed many generations of exceptional, productive and balanced individuals all over the world. Be good to yourself and to your kids.

FAME & THE FARM

Let us not give up meeting together, as some are in the habit of doing, but let us encourage one another—and all the more as you see the Day approaching. Hebrews 10:25

WHEN MY KIDS WERE GROWING UP, FOR SOME REASON THEY CORRELATED THE IMAGE OF LIMOUSINES WITH FAME. The dark-tinted windows of these stretch vehicles always made them ask the same question: "I wonder which famous person is in there?" Then they would jokingly start their wish list of who they thought might be hidden behind those shady windows. In quiet amazement, I realized there was a reason for their infatuation—the hope of accomplishment and of sharing that success with others. Years later, when a limo picked us up at the airport at the same rate that a taxi cab would charge, both girls stuck their heads out of the sunroof! "We don't want people to have to guess who is in here," they said. "That just makes it miserable for everybody who is *not* in here."

So quickly the image of stardom and royalty converted to commonality but still with a sense of pride. Never again did I hear, "I wonder which famous person is in there?" In our dreams we all belong there. And in reality, we are all there. In today's world of social media that is so puzzling to me, but also so pretty and enthusiastic, we lift the veil of the limo. Everybody is sticking their heads out of the sunroof with posts that say, "Look, it's me. Look where I am. Look how fortunate I am. Look how happy we are." And suddenly happiness is where it always belonged. Right where I am and exactly who we are.

I see this happiness and unbridled satisfaction every day in the vineyards right here at Kiepersol. I know that it is for us a workplace and a farming lifestyle, but for many others it's a much-needed moment of connection with earth, beauty and purity seemingly as mythical as the famous person in the limousine.

My Parents' Forever Child

Not looking to your own interests but each of you to the interests of others. Philippians 2:4

IN HIS IMAGE, WE EXPECT PEOPLE TO BE. Generation after generation, we have that expectation that all people are created equal. But Jesus said, "Let the little children come to me and do not hinder them for the Kingdom of Heaven belongs to such as these." (Mark 10:14) In the last couple of weeks our Forever Children are constantly on my mind. Those we expected, when we expected them, to be "the next little me." But they're created different. They behave different. They act different. They need different things. But they truly live like we need to live. They are always ready to give hugs because they need hugs. They are excited to tell stories because they want to hear stories. They have no pretentious moments or ungrounded fears. They trust when others tremble. Their truths know no lies. They have a place in heaven because they have the knowledge of good, but see and hear no evil. Yes, they are precious Forever Kids who need the things children need … forever. But the years age their bones and bodies. Their hair also turns gray. The ones who love and care at some time pass away.

We love and praise the winners, the smart ones and the achievers. And it is to all of you I write this tonight because we were in the front of the line, and that position in life comes with obligations. To share and to care. To give security and dignity to those aging children who can never bring it to themselves, those who have an unwavering trust that tomorrow will again be a sunny day.

This Friday night at Bushman's Celebration Center you can meet some of them. It is auditing time. Count your blessings and come and share them. They need them—they need you—they need me. They need us to care because they are our blessings. When you know one, you know all; you know what innocence means, what innocence does and what innocence needs. If you can't make it to Bushman's, discover a residential home for Forever Children like Breckenridge Village or a non-profit like Mane Mission and bless yourself by giving richly. I know the caregivers at Breckenridge Village, and on behalf of all of you, I thank them for their everlasting patience and the love and care they so generously share with those created for heaven.

If you know blessed people, share this with them.

It's Not Just the Wine. It's the Place.

How good and pleasant it is when God's people live together in unity! Psalm 133:1

I CAN'T BELIEVE IT IS ALREADY THE SECOND WEEK IN OCTOBER. Another year that just disappeared on us. I guess it is because we stay busy, and we like what we do. Seems like when you like what you do, and you like who is around you, suddenly you realize how many wonderful people are around.

Here at the winery, it is almost as if there are "Austin weekends." Last weekend was "San Antonio weekend." This weekend was "Beaumont weekend." Every weekend is a wonderful mix of people from all over, but it's a little bit more memorable when so many people from a certain area make themselves acquainted. This weekend I got to meet the happy smile of Nicholas, now one of my favorite Forever Children. You meet so many people, and by Sunday morning you've got the images of all of them stored away, but names and where they are from, in some cases, dissipate overnight.

But somehow we know they'll be back. We'll see them in a month or two, or we'll see them at their next anniversary. They come to become a part of something: a kinship, a place where different people find commonality. No, the commonality is not only based on wine or food. It is based on the need for nature, nostalgia and knowledge. It is part of the search in each of us for the better things in life. Not more money, not more stuff—just a better frame of mind. Something that's near and neighborly, an hour or two or ten of positive displacement of society's rat race. An urge to get away from the TV, the news, the sports and the phone—everything that is drowning all of us slowly but surely. We trade business cards, not for business' sake, but in an attempt to extend the genuineness of the moment. And at the end of the weekend on our wine farm, we simply reflect and realize how blessed we are for those who have truly come and enriched both their souls and ours.

IS GOODNESS A YEARNING?

But the fruit of the Spirit is love, joy, peace, forbearance, kindness, goodness, faithfulness, gentleness and self-control.
Galatians 5:22-23

I'M STANDING AT THE CHECKOUT COUNTER LOOKING AT THIS RED-HAIRED, HAPPY-FACED YOUNG GIRL PACKING THE GROCERIES. A little bit loud. I know why she is always packing and someone else is running the cash register. Does she ever get the acknowledgment we all yearn for? At the car when everything was diligently packed together, one of the handles broke on a sack. "Be careful," I said. "You are my favorite person at Brookshire's." And her whole demeanor lit up. So proud and so acknowledged. I've seen her there for a year or more, but I suddenly felt delinquent in this acknowledgment.

It made my mind run back to yesterday at the Men's Breakfast and Car Show benefitting Breckenridge Village. Year after year, once a year, we get reminded of God's phenomenal way of blending happiness and pain into the perfect instruction of responsibility, opportunity and duty. Grandma always said real men could shed a tear. It is only a sign that their throat got closed. Yesterday 80-plus closed-throated men experienced the power of positive acknowledgment. They realized blessings don't look the same, feel the same or act the same. They are God-given, and whatever God has done in His creations, He always says, "It is good." So finding purpose and acceptance is our task. I see car lovers leave mild and solemn when three hours earlier they had arrived with vroom, vroom and rev, rev. Every one of us left there with the full intention to be better, to love more, to be kinder and to be a little less self-absorbed with our needs and wants.

I've always heard what you sow, you will reap. My life has been so blessed, and in many cases I reaped long before I had the capacity to sow. My question is, how do we turn that roomful of old men into a roomful of young men who have years of sowing ahead? God bless our Forever Children and those who care so diligently.

GLORIOUS SUNSETS

From the rising of the sun to the place where it sets, the name of the Lord is to be praised. Psalm 113:3

I ALWAYS SAID THE WEATHER IS WHAT THE LORD WANTS US TO HAVE. And whatever that is, I'm happy with it. Lord, am I happy for these last three sunny days. Days like today are what make Texas a paradise in January. It is true: sunlight brings happiness. The vines, even in their dormant stage, have a beauty about them when the sun shines brightly and a light breeze makes everything seem alive. Weekends are a "time-share"—time enjoying our loyal Kiepersol visitors, answering their questions and sharing our place. And it is with great gratitude that I reflect on what is happening here.

Our growing tribe is as diverse as our state and our country. All people with a hankering for what is local, knowledge of how it's made and appreciation for the seasons that were captured. From judges to doctors, nurses to CEOs and valets to farmers—all are together enjoying what they consider their own. It is clean and it is pure, and it's in the true fashion of sharing that people come and enjoy, take possession and time after time bring new friends to share our wine farm. All I can say is thank you. It is you we care about, and it is you we want to please. Nothing is overly luxurious; it is just our farmer's way of giving you the best we can dream of, afford and share. Know you are loved and appreciated and that we always want you to leave happy. And if you do, help us grow the tribe. We'll take good care of all. After all, what is better than good company, a good adult beverage and a glorious sunset?

When the Height of the Blue Skies Is Your Only Limitation

Do your best to present yourself to God as one approved, a worker who does not need to be ashamed and who correctly handles the word of truth. 2 Timothy 2:15

I DON'T KNOW IF IT WAS EVER DIFFERENT. But it sure feels as if there is a war on work ... physical work. The nature of farm work has always been environmental: hot days, cold days, wet days, dry days. For me, every one of those days came with a satisfaction that I did it, I liked it and I achieved some coherent synchronization with nature. I hear every day of people with degrees and education who cannot find a job. And if they have one, don't like their job. We don't pay minimum wage; we pay a little bit better. If you hang in there, I believe there are satisfying careers for the right people in agriculture. I don't know if it is social welfare that is changing working hands into taking hands or if it is the "coolness" factor. Is farm work not cool today? I know it's not the physical exertion that is of concern because people pay to go into air-conditioned environments and physically exert themselves to the sweat-dripping point. I'm not talking about only grunt work. I'm talking about operators, technicians, cellar people ... jobs that are not always out in the elements.

Is our industry so small that people don't know or never hear about the satisfaction that comes with it? The satisfaction of seasonal transformation—fruit in an embryonic state developing right in your hands and in front of your eyes into maturity? The awesome experience of a sky full of bright sunlight being swallowed by cottony clouds covering the heavens, then turning dark and breaking open into a refreshing shower? Being outside where you can see a dive-bombing bird of prey or the hurried swiggle of a lizard running away? It's not just work—it's organic, it's nature, it's knowledge. It's knowing that the breeze changed directions and that something in the weather is going to change. It's getting soaking wet with the cleanest clean water. It's getting home and rinsing off the dust with a satisfying nod of the head ... it was a long day. It's a job everybody envies but nobody wants to do. It's a career that those trapped in their rat race at old age desire too late. I think all of us who can find a way to work the land and make a living out of it are blessed. Why is it so hard to convince people of the blessings that come with the land?

He Saw the Vine

May the God of hope fill you with all joy and peace as you trust in him, so that you may overflow with hope by the power of the Holy Spirit. Romans 15:13

WHAT A WONDERFUL WEEKEND WITH FAMILY AND FRIENDS. Not only counting blessings but also expressing sincere thankfulness for the times, people and the places you don't always think of. Another Thanksgiving full of firsts. The first time somebody special is not there. The first Thanksgiving with a new little one or two. Thanksgiving is where we can say, "Thank you for ... " So many blessings we have. Today at the winery we had a guest who was 100 years old. He was so thankful that he could experience a vineyard and a winery in East Texas. I'm so thankful that he could experience it here. Like he said, East Texas is beautiful, but this makes it feel like a different world—one I only dreamed of. He said, "I'm a Christian man, and I love the stories of the vine. Today I could touch it."

The weather has been beautiful and the sunrises and sunsets so brilliant and full of hope, highlighting this season of joy. Before we know it, Christmas will be upon us. And then the whole new beginning of a new year. Seasons are coming and going, and we live in a free fall. Our time is consumed by the irrelevant things that we cannot change, when relevance and joy is within our reach, ready for the taking. Make this season yours. Find reasons to smile. Smother those negative vibes. Be joyful. Get lost in place and forget about yourself. If you do, this season might just be the stimulation for a life full of joy and appreciation for the beautiful and majestic minutes of happiness that can turn into hours, days, weeks and years.

CONGRATULATIONS

In all your ways submit to him, and he will make your paths straight. Proverbs 3:6

VOICEMAILS, ANSWERING MACHINES AND RECEPTIONISTS. In the process of everybody chasing social media for their business expansion, dreams and sales, they neglect the basics. This morning I went on the Internet and found the product that I needed. The website gave a phone number, hours of operation and the time zone. When I called the number, a friendly receptionist answered the phone, asked politely what I needed and told me to hold for a second so she could see if the right person was in. A very friendly salesperson then answered the phone, called me by my name and was excited to help me with a $59 purchase. Efficient, cordial and precise. Congratulations,

Steve Davis—you are the kind of person who needs a promotion! You are the kind of person who almost doesn't exist anymore, and you are the kind of person who takes care of the details that make business work.

One out of 20 places I call today will be an answering machine asking me to leave a message and a phone number. I will call again later today and again maybe tomorrow—every time leaving the same message. Somebody in marketing, somebody managing social media: from time to time, just try to get in touch with your company. See how in vain your pursuit of new business is. We will also try to improve.

CHAPTER SEVEN
SOCIETY

REPETITION CAN BE MAKE-BELIEVE

*A cheerful heart is good medicine, but a crushed spirit
dries up the bones. Proverbs 17:22*

MOST OF US ARE TRYING TO BE REASONABLY IN TUNE
WITH WHAT IS HAPPENING AROUND US AND AROUND
THE WORLD. We live on news—stories, tales and promotions
that spin in a repetitious fashion that creates anxiety. An
anxiety that destabilizes the base of our existence. Like
forgiveness, hopes and dreams are deliberate and intentional
emotions. As farmers, we cannot live in fear and doom and
gloom. We have to live the day, praise the blessings and do
the duties that keep us whole. This week reconfirmed to
me that our world is not as big as people make it, and our

dreams are bigger than our world. Our hopes are rooted in our duty. And our happiness is close to home. Live a little, laugh a lot and enjoy today because you can.

WHO WON THIS ROUND?

I appeal to you, brothers and sisters, in the name of our Lord Jesus Christ, that all of you agree with one another in what you say and that there be no divisions among you, but that you be perfectly united in mind and thought.
1 Corinthians 1:10

IT WAS THE BIG WEEK. The mid-term elections. Where everybody thinks that half the people are idiots. It doesn't matter where you stand or what you believe. With great anticipation millions of dollars were spent (half on idiots) to still be a divided people. In hindsight it is sad that we can live these dichotomies so vividly. We hate immigrants because they might vote, but we don't vote. We build churches on every corner in every town, but as a Christian country we won't vote and support our belief system. Even if you don't believe, you still have knowledge of good and bad, and you should vote for what is good. Half of us cannot be all wrong. We always discuss what we want, but we never discuss what we need to do. Maybe when we discuss that, we can accept small steps in the right direction and get small pieces of freedom returned to the people. I understand that not everybody has the desire for the *same* freedoms, but I know we all have the desire for freedom.

If we ran our businesses with people and managers like we elect, we'll be financially broke. I've never experienced life as just a give or take. It is a constant evaluation, negotiation and a diligent process where we sometimes make mistakes. But by taking care of the details we can usually correct them before they are disasters. I strongly believe in "we the people" being made in an image of the Great Designer. A people set free by great love and put into bondage by great fear. We'll talk about this again and again, and as long as I can remember we have talked about it. But the pundits plant lust, fear and horror as everyday talking points in our way. We are so caught up in the big do-goods or do-bads that we can never see or experience the details of our conscience ourselves.

I say the birthplace of big government is somewhere in small-town USA. Small seeds grow big weeds. And small freedoms sacrificed become big dreams crushed. Not all of us are blessed with the wisdom of Solomon, but it is so hard to follow the wise when they have mouths bigger than their brains. The biggest noisemakers become the leaders. And the biggest promise-makers never had the means to fulfill or execute their promises. So for me it comes down to the simple, small details. What do I *not* want done to me, and why would I do it to others? Personally, I've reaped love and kindness long before I knew to sow love and kindness. I've reaped freedom that was so sweet that it makes me want to sow freedom. Shouldn't we?

Freedom is what we yearn for. Freedom to be exactly what we can be. But freedom has never been free from responsibility. It is clear to me that as we have shunned our responsibilities, we have sacrificed our freedoms. As long as we look for someone else to blame or someone else to do, we'll increase the have-to-dos and decrease the want-to-dos. It took a long time to encumber this free nation, but as the encumbrance grows exponentially, we have to realize that no law or rule or regulation ever sets us free. It only enhances the pace whereby we stifle our American exceptionalism. And when we accept that we are not exceptional and the sky is not the limit and we are not free, we lose our glow and glory and hope. I'll never lose hope because I believe half of us are brilliant.

COMPETITIVE TOGETHERNESS

If the part of the dough offered as first fruits is holy, then the whole batch is holy; if the root is holy, so are the branches. Romans 11:16

WE HEAR A LOT ABOUT "TOO BIG TO FAIL," BUT NOBODY EVER TALKS ABOUT THE UNITY OF LOCAL INDUSTRY. Small units in the same industry can never become too big to fail if they are honest and united in their competition with themselves and not with each other. Good, positive representation of an industry helps everybody in that industry. If you have to build your brand by tearing down other brands, you just lower yours to the same level you put others. Tough economic times create the exact climate for industry enhancement.

This can go for any small industry. As the Texas wine industry, we have to identify the two or three attributes that we all have in common, that we're all proud of and that we all agree on disclosing to everyone in the state and in the world. Every winery, every vineyard and every winemaker can proudly represent a piece of the body of the Texas wine industry—only after accepting the attributes of every other piece of the body necessary for survival.

Kiepersol is a part of Tyler. Kiepersol is a part of the Texas wine industry. Everything we represent is local.

CHAPTER EIGHT
GENERATIONS

Younger Sets of Hands

Don't let anyone look down on you because you are young,
but set an example for the believers in speech, in conduct,
in love, in faith and in purity. 1 Timothy 4:12

NOT ONLY IS IT OFFICIALLY SPRING, BUT EVERYTHING LOOKS AND FEELS LIKE IT IS SPRING—THAT SEASON OF ENTHUSIASM, NEW HOPE, NEW BEGINNINGS AND YOUTHFULNESS. The Hill Country Wine Symposium gave me that same spring feeling. Excited young people, bright-eyed and full of dreams and the plans and energy to execute them. An experience very rare in my field of agriculture.

You always hear that farming is aging and becoming one of the industries with the least amount of entrants, embittered by the seasons and numbed by the regulators.

But today I saw something different.

I saw dreams that are free and people who want to connect with the land. I saw young men and women hungry for hope being receptive to the task their dreams will bring. People who dream of an industry of labor and sweat, of dust and dirt, of sun and rain and cold that hopefully, in time, turns into precious Texas wine. Hands that face downward, not looking for a gift—just a chance to make their spring young, dream their dreams and do their thing. Young people stepping out of the box and shooting a root into a beautiful Texas way of loving, learning and living. My dream for them is to have as little governmental interference as possible and to be left alone to fail or succeed on their own. What I see at Kiepersol, and what I saw at the symposium, gives me hope and pride. It makes me believe that this is not only the spring season but also the spring of the wine industry in Texas with a vengeance and vigor.

WHAT'S NEXT?

"For I know the plans I have for you," declares the Lord,
"plans to prosper you and not to harm you, plans to give
you hope and a future." Jeremiah 29:11

NOT TOO LONG AGO, MY KIDS WERE ASKING, "ARE WE ALMOST THERE?" Not so long before them, I was the one who asked, "Are we almost there?" So it is not really a new generation thing, this instant gratification. Everything is live—everything is happening right now and everybody needs to know what I'm doing right now. That's what "they" say. I'm sure you are the center of your world, just as we thought we were the center of ours. But still today, like then, who actually cares?

I've been pondering this and looking at young people putting on a smile for a selfie with the beautiful vineyard behind them. And I beg to differ with what "they" say. Here on the wine farm, everybody is the center of our world. We can't make everybody happy, but we're trying. We want you to say, "I've been there." Or ask, "When are we going again?" and "How can we get there faster?" Come see us and let us spoil you.

WHEN THE STRONG
BECOME FRAIL

*The heart of the discerning acquires knowledge, for the
ears of the wise seek it out. Proverbs 18:15*

IT'S A VICIOUS, WELL-DESERVED CYCLE. Many times I
ponder the thought of knowledge transfer, or better said,
experience transfer. Hardheaded as I am, I've gotten most
of my knowledge by experience—almost as if that is the
only knowledge that really sinks in. But when the icons
in our sphere mature past a ripe old age, the reality of that
knowledge base expiring becomes obviously certain. The
bigger the icon, the more impossible to find a mind big
enough to clone the years of wisdom earned. I don't dwell
on the negative, because retirement is a well-deserved time

when the constant flares and signals of daily dos and don'ts no longer have to light up anymore. It is a deserving time for everyone to just look back and say, "It was good."

I can't help but sometimes wonder what my father, Dirk, would have said or done. And then I wonder, *Why did I squander precious time chasing frivolous pursuits?*

Instead of philosophizing over a glass of perfect East Texas red wine.

Instead of smoking a handmade cigar.

Instead of storing away the wisdom of times gone by for the questions of a time not yet here.

When steps and breaths become short, stop, listen and take in the wisest words because they will be the last clear messages to those of us who want to listen. History is today. And if we are endowed with tomorrow, today's lesson might be the perfectly placed wisdom for the unforeseen challenge. Admire the wise and love the frail. Enhance all those you touch with intellectual capital that will otherwise expire. We never get too old to learn. We just need to learn who to learn from.

Those who are blessed to become frail deserve a loving, kind and inquiring mind with whom to share the finer things and thoughts that make tomorrow a better day for all.

BEEN THERE, DONE THAT

Now faith is being sure of what we hope for and certain of what we do not see. Hebrews 11:1

A S THE YEARS GROW AND THE WISDOM MULTIPLIES, THE TOLERANCE FOR RISK DIMINISHES. It takes a real man or woman to look back in hindsight at their successes and see that none were risk-free. There comes a day when you have to look at the young 'uns and say, "Go for it." Go for it with the same enthusiasm, spirit and hard work that you created your own wisdom with. Because it is not transferable without the risk.

I don't know exactly when you lose tolerance for risk. But what I know for sure is that the greatest generation was the greatest *before* they had experience and wisdom. They had love, passion, dreams and "want to." And they were willing to get up and fall down . . . and get up, fall down and get up again.

I personally live in a bubble where my dearest friends are the wise men of our community. They are people who calculated risks that were not calculable. They are people who made it when others failed. They are the people who hand over the reins at the right time, to the right people. They are the people who took chances on people. And at times they were disappointed, but they were very successful.

The future looks brighter despite what you read or watch. The young ones are smarter than or at least as smart as the brightest of us. They are proud and have dreams. Maybe their skills are the same as ours, but the knowledge pool is so instant and the world is so transparent that they attack their goals with laser-sharp energy in ways we never could. Do yourself a favor. Look around and just see the quality and integrity of those who are taking the reins. Those who are leading the way. Those who look at the now-transparent risks that were hidden from us. I'm proud of getting older, but I'm more proud of those who can wake up, stand up, look up and perform. The next generation is going to make us proud.

It's Only Dust

May God give you heaven's dew and earth's richness—an abundance of grain and new wine. Genesis 27:28

THERE'S SOMETHING ABOUT PEOPLE WHO ENJOY THE FINER THINGS IN LIFE THAT IS SO ABSOLUTELY AWESOME. The finer things in life normally go with the highest standards of sanitation, cleaning, hygiene, labels and notoriety. But all that disappears and excitement takes over whenever you pull an old dust-covered and stained bottle of wine from the cellar. Suddenly that dust takes us to those good old days. That "wow"—that special occasion, that special year. That's when we realize we are dust to dust. We have to have that contact with earth. There's earth in the bottle, seasons captured, memories and dates. There is a connection with the land that no other product can bring but wine. There is an anticipation and a sigh of relief when the cork is not soft. And when you pour, you know it's old, but we call it "wonderfully mature." We swirl and we sniff, expecting those memories, that year or that season to come back. And it does. It comes back because Dad was still alive or Grandpa was still farming. That's the year of graduation, of dumbness and youngness and numbness. But those memories take you to a date, a place and a taste … now made more special because it has faded, bringing forth only the good. Everyone has dreams for the future, but the happy ties to the past are what forever last only in wine, the dated offering from the land. Break out a bottle, compare it with the new. Make good memories today that will never fade.

CHAPTER NINE
PEACE

Just Be

Peace I leave with you; my peace I give you. I do not give to you as the world gives. Do not let your hearts be troubled and do not be afraid. John 14:27

WHILE OTHER ORGANIZATIONS ARE BUILDING ON EVENTS AND SPECIAL OCCASIONS TO BRING IN CUSTOMERS, I FEEL A LITTLE COMPELLED TO REBEL. On a recent vacation I did absolutely nothing … I just *was*. Sure, there were lots of activities available—scuba diving, whale watching, parasailing or shopping at the hot spots in the city. I chose none of those. I thought I'd catch up on some reading by the pool instead. I fired up the Kindle, but the Wi-Fi was intermittent at best and of course I hadn't actually downloaded any of my books from the cloud. I felt panicked and a little trapped in paradise. What was happening at the office, and who am I missing on the brand's Facebook page? Then it washed over me. I need this peace. I don't deserve it, but in some ways I need it. I couldn't remember the last time I had my own thoughts without Googling to confirm something or to see what someone else had already thought about it.

Admittedly, I did buy *The Alchemist* in the gift shop for some attempt at entertainment, but I put it down after several hours. I felt as if it was saying, "The meaning of life is coming up … it's in this book, just around the corner." Well intentioned, but don't we all want to discover that for ourselves in our own time? Is it really that simple? If I told you what the key to happiness is, would you believe me if you hadn't experienced it? So I had a few more mango smoothies (they make one with a vanilla tequila, oh my) and was back on track with the thought of just "being."

The restoration we all need is a place to just be ourselves. The setting was not necessarily quiet, with waves continually crashing as a backdrop and the occasional crying child with sunblock in his eye. But it just took a little mind-shift for all of that to become part of the bliss. What I realized when I got back was that Kiepersol is just such a place too. I can walk through the vineyard and simply let thoughts float about. I can eat at the restaurant and not be rushed by a waiter or bombarded by boom-boom music (I think you know what I mean) or herded like cattle to my table. I can soak in the season and just enjoy friends. I found a special place close to home, and I hope you discover that Kiepersol can be a restorative place for you too.

WHAT CROSS DO YOU BEAR?

A gentle tongue is a tree of life, but perverseness in it breaks the spirit. Proverbs 15:4

WHY DO WE ASK, "HOW ARE YOU?" As if we expect some good news, some happiness, some positive vibes or something we didn't expect. A dear friend passed away a couple of weeks ago. In the midst of his battle with cancer, he sent a vibe of enthusiastic peacefulness. Under his circumstances, this was unexpected even though I knew he was already a very positive person. A positive mind that directs truthful lips only exists in those who understand the biblical concept that the words you utter will come true. I think the perpetual whining and tiredness you encounter when you ask some people how they are doing is very seldom to never due to performing physical or strenuous labor. Instead it's the vicious cycle of negative expression that never leaves them. Because what they speak comes true. My friend said, "I'm wonderful." And it came true. I know where he is.

JUST BE STILL

Greater love has no one than this: to lay down one's life for one's friends. John 15:13

EVERY DAY IS MEMORIAL DAY FOR SOMEBODY. Tomorrow is Memorial Day for everybody. Can't help but think of a platoon somewhere in a war zone hearing the thumps of a non-recoil three-barrel mortar. Then hearing the whistle and the first mortar hitting just left of them and the second just right of them. Then knowing that the last one will be in the middle of them. One yell, "God, help us." Because they know where the third one will land. And it lands, but it doesn't explode. Right smack dab in the middle of them.

Old men picked the fights. Young men made the sacrifices. And everywhere mothers stayed in teary prayer every living moment.

Somewhere in the Pacific a torpedo pilot is diving down on the enemy, and he knows it is skill versus skill, training versus training, experience versus experience. But ultimately, it's a greater hand with a greater purpose that prevails as he completes his mission with a roar to safety.

There were times when the whole nation was affected by war. There were times when some of the nation was affected by war. And there were times when very few in the nation were affected by war. But it is still a war, decided by old men to preserve our internal freedoms. Freedoms that those same men in so many cases dilute with regulations and constraints. The old men move on, and the young men get old. And some never serve. And some never know.

One Memorial Day will come where everybody will have fun, and no one will know who made the sacrifices for that day's beer and barbecue. Remember, freedom came at a very dear price. Just reflect and be still in thought and prayer because somebody fought for your share.

IT WAS THAT KIND OF WEEKEND

You will keep in perfect peace those whose minds are steadfast, because they trust in you. Isaiah 26:3

A WEEKEND WHERE YOU FELT TRAPPED WITH GLADNESS THAT YOU CAN BE INSIDE—SAFE, SECURE AND COMFORTABLE. It was that kind of weekend when you were glad you didn't have to put up the Christmas lights. When you postponed going to buy things in town that you thought you needed but can really do without. It truly was a weekend when you could open a bottle of Kiepersol wine and feel and taste the summer and the glorious Texas weather and what it produced. It is truly awesome how that season in the bottle can keep you warm, happy and satisfied on a weekend like that.

THE BEAUTY AND THE BEAST OF SILENCE

People listened to me expectantly, waiting in silence for my counsel. Job 29:21

WE GET SO BOMBARDED WITH NOISE. Noisy news ... other people's views ... other people's opinions ... other people's wars. Cell phones and emails, texts, and for some of us, even faxes. That silence at the end of the day or at the end of the week is so precious. That silence that goes with the East Texas sunset, a glass of wine and just being— dreaming off in the distance—makes it all bearable. But don't let our desire to have quiet and peace make us silent. I don't get political and don't want to be political. But as Americans (or should I just start with "us Texans"?), don't let us lose our voice. I believe that the majority of us Democrats, Republicans or whatever are all losing our rights and freedoms at a pace I've never seen ... because we are silent.

Over the years I knew those who talk normally don't do anything. And those that do something don't talk. But our talkers today talk out of both sides of their mouths. And the louder they talk, the more silent we get. It is amazing to me that everybody I know wants the same. They want to be free to pursue dreams, free to make decisions, free to take risks, free to fail, free to succeed and free to choose. No one I know has the intent or desire to hurt or act unjustly. But a small group of radicals on every side of every issue has the voices today. Bullies who stop at nothing to create misery, fear and guilt with everyone who's not boisterous.

I've heard people say they have a sixth sense—something like intuition or a gut feeling. Good for them. All I ask is that you use your common sense. If the rule is good for the goose, it should be good for the gander; and if you don't need a rule, even better. Take responsibility for yourself and for those who value the freedoms that we're giving up every day. Wake up, stand up, get up, go to work; build your own dreams and your own destiny. It's not muscles and mouth that maketh a man but patience, wisdom and a voice of reason. Ask the good Lord for wisdom, and surround yourself with the wise.

We, the majority of Americans, have to speak up. We have to say enough is enough. And no more talk. We need to find doers who can dismantle the burdens and the minefields of regulations, rules and obligations we have to crawl through in order to live our dreams. Yes, we used to be free, and it is almost just the dreams of that freedom that are left. And we, the silent majority, feed the monster of big government to devour us and we don't even know it anymore. It's time to not be silent. Our silence will be the end of the "shining city on the hill."

REBOOT

Come to me, all you who are weary and burdened, and I will give you rest. Matthew 11:28

I SN'T REBOOTING THE MOST AWESOME, EASY WAY TO HAVE A CORRECTIVE ACTION? My definition of a reboot is rethinking the enterprise, the sequence and the purpose. Reboot is so prevalent in our society but so unintentional in our everyday lives. I heard someone say, "I have to come to the vineyard to reboot and get my values and priorities in the correct sequence." And then at sunset the skies above the vineyard came alive, along with the dronelike hovering of thousands of dragonflies over the vineyard celebrating the end of harvest and the beginning of the end of the season. It's as if they know the vineyard will naturally reboot. The season will come, and the season will go. And before we know it, the next one will be prettier and better than those we knew before.

We understand so much and apply so little. Do we ever take time to stop? I mean stop and just think. What are we doing, and why are we doing it? Our lives are like a hurricane building—a never-ending spiral of have-tos, need-tos, must-dos that are in the end meaningless. When you look in hindsight at that almost out of control, unbalanced existence, you know that rebooting was long overdue. Change your environment to work with you instead of against you. It is time to reboot everything. Planning, rules, regulations, obligations, priorities and sometimes people and associations—especially pretentious do-good politicians. We can't live in storms every day. We have to have sunlight and showers so that we can take responsibility for ourselves in every aspect of our existence. And yet we must still understand there is only one hand we can depend on, the calm and steady hand of our Lord and Savior.

CHAPTER TEN
TEXAS

FIELD HANDS Mindful Stories from the Fields of Life

Texan by Choice

*You did not choose me, but I chose you and appointed
you so that you might go and bear fruit—fruit that will
last—and so that whatever you ask in my name the
Father will give you. John 15:16*

I'M NOT ONE TO BE INFLUENCED BY NEGATIVE VIBES.
I'm blessed with my outlook on life and blessed by
the people surrounding me at Kiepersol who are positive,
happy, self-confident and honest people. I'm Texan and
American by choice. I just want to say that when you don't
know anything else, you might not realize how wonderful
a place Texas is. You may not recognize the wonderful
opportunities that this great state offers. Don't squander our
freedom and hide behind our Texas name, pride, labels and
product if it is not truly Texas. Cheers!

The River Pour

Be wise in the way you act toward outsiders; make the most of every opportunity. Colossians 4:5

ON SUNDAY NIGHT WE HEADED HOME FROM SAN ANTONIO, WHERE WE POURED WINE AT THE RED CARPET EVENTS OF THE 20ᵀᴴ SAN ANTONIO FILM FESTIVAL. We feel honored that they selected Kiepersol wine as their Texas wine of choice. And it truly was two evenings of *wows* and *oohs* and *ahhs* about our wine. Moviemakers, stars, scriptwriters and VIPs from all over the country enjoyed and complimented our East Texas wine. By now I know when somebody is just kind and when it is a real compliment. But this weekend it was easy to tell the difference when they kept coming back for more. It is so crazy that people can ship all kinds of stuff from all over the world, but to everyone who asks if we can ship to New York or L.A. or New Orleans, I have to say, "no." Not every Texas business has the same right to commerce, e-commerce and interstate shipping.

We met lots of wonderful people, most of whom were city people, movie people. A little different than our everyday tasting room and winery client. I myself haven't been to a movie theater since *Crocodile Dundee* came out in the mid-1980s. Even on TV it is hard for me to find entertainment that is wholesome and happy enough to keep my attention without being weird and absurd. While heading down to San Antonio I initially contemplated an unenjoyable trip with people so different from me. I almost dreaded the journey. But those who weren't wine lovers didn't drink. And those who were wine lovers were just our kind. I don't know why I expected the movie crowd's wine drinkers to be different than our wine drinkers, but I did.

San Antonio, we enjoyed being there with you. You are one of Texas' prettiest cities, and your people look like Texas. What was more obvious there than in any place I've been lately is the amount of families—parents and kids— out on the street or at the movies just being everywhere together. That makes your city even prettier for me. Thank you for the open arms. We were proud to be present in your city. The more you ask for, the more we'll give.

Texas Pride

*Let us not become weary in doing good, for at the
proper time we will reap a harvest if we do not give up.*
Galatians 6:9

How quickly 16 years has gone by. Kiepersol's
vines and winery just turned 16, and finally we can
say "Happy Sweet Sixteen." When I go in the library and I
taste some of the first wines, I know this was a long road of
improvement. As the vines matured, so did the winemakers
and our industry. I want to say thank you to everybody who
walked this road with us. Especially the other Texas wineries
that are also improving and diligently promoting what we
as Texans can do. I know all of us sometimes feel we are on
this wine island alone, fighting the imports and the mass
merchandisers. But the love for what we do and everyone's

endurance have brought us to a point where I hear every weekend how proud people are of what we as an industry have done over the years.

Our local following is getting stronger. Bloggers, writers and competitions are much more positive. And what I always knew is now reality ... our destiny is our Texas destination. There is a Texas wine and a winery for all. I got to know and taste a lot of Texas wines during the KE Cellars years when we had storefront locations in Tyler, and we promoted those wines as hard as our own. Thanks to the efforts and pride of all the Texas winemakers, we have become internationally known as a true wine producing state.

The season was good and mild, and up until now the weather was just a blend of fall, fog and phenomenal days. We can just wish that it lasts. Again, thank you to everyone in our industry, our phenomenal fans and our proud Texas consumers. This is to you, with wishes for a blessed Christmas season and prosperity in the New Year. And if the season makes you gain weight, I hope it is all in faith.

CHAPTER ELEVEN
GROWING

GROWTH

For the kingdom of heaven is like a landowner who went
out early in the morning to hire workers for his vineyard.
Matthew 20:1

I T'S AMAZING TO ME HOW GROWTH, THE IGNITER OF
PROSPERITY, IS REGULATED BY PEOPLE WHO DO NOT WANT
OTHERS TO PROSPER. It is unbelievable that so many in
today's "control thy neighbor" society have no idea, concept
or perspective of the evolution of societal prosperity. As I
look at our vineyards, I see the humble, poor-boy beginnings.
The stepping-stone approaches. The "enhance when you can"
and "improve when you have to" mindset to maintain image
and growth. I know that Kiepersol Estates Vineyards would
not have existed if I had planned at day one for it to look and
be structured the way it is today.

There's a very proud evolutionary process that took place as we started to crawl, then walk and then run. Hopefully we're not mature yet. But most of those who are in constant pursuit of controlling what others do (e.g., controlling others' ability to make a living, think freely, dream skyward and create legacies) feel powerful enough in their own minuscule existence of constraints and equalization to leave a legacy as empty as their heads for generations to come!

New Vistas

Forget the former things; do not dwell on the past.
Isaiah 43:18

After a wet/dry election we saw the changes of a freer people in parts of Smith County. KE Cellars ceased to be the only location where closed containers of adult beverages like wine could be purchased. Dozens of new locations became licensed, and thousands of selections entered our market. That brought us choice, competition and responsibilities. I always said competition makes us stronger and makes us work harder to stay the best.

I want to commend the Kiepersol team for standing their ground as I expected. In the international wine arena not only have they proven that East Texas can produce a wine that can stand with the biggest and the most prestigious, but also they created a destination where locals can proudly entertain guests and where people from all over the world can enjoy a true Texas estate wine.

At KE Cellars we brought the estate wine to the people, but in the last year we have seen a phenomenal increase in people coming to the estate. We made sure the wine is available at multiple locations in East Texas and even throughout the rest of Texas. The end of this month will be the end of an era at KE Cellars. Thanks to all the proud patrons, we outgrew the little tasting room and its facilities at the winery on the estate. We are in the process of enhancing your destination experience with a brand new tasting room overlooking the original vineyards in the serene style that only cowboys and *vinifera* can create. Come see, come enjoy and stay Texas proud ... we are.

CHAPTER TWELVE
CLOSER TO THE HEART

THE GREAT ESCAPE

Do everything in love. 1 Corinthians 16:14

Is it a once a year thing, or is it a once a year reminder that it is an everyday thing? It's Valentine's and love is in the air. It's anniversaries and weddings, date night and treating each other like you always want to be treated. But remember, it's hands down a day where we enjoy all the privileges of Valentine's because of our soldiers, our law enforcement people and those who will spend this day and evening protecting your Valentine's rights while being away from their own valentines. This Valentine's, love yourself first ... and then love the ones you love like you love yourself.

For many, this will be a lonesome day. Maybe a painful reminder of lost ones and lost opportunities. For many, this will be a new day with new promises, new responsibilities and new opportunities to sow what they want to reap. It is a day when you can put things in perspective and love what you have and not what you want. Touch those who are close and truly are your neighbors. Think of those who paved your way with perfect examples of love and who had dreams that *yours* would be better than *theirs*. Valentine's is not only for the young and beautiful; it is a day when everybody can say, "I love you."

The Valentine's escapes already started last weekend with perfect weather bringing serenity to the vineyards and our visitors. If I heard it one time in the last week, I've heard it 30 times ... Kiepersol is the "perfect escape" from the things we have to do to the things we love to do. At Kiepersol we love you. Have a blessed Valentine's Day. Be safe, drink responsibly and be good to yourself and others. And if you need to escape, we'll be here like always to make your day a better day.

PUPPY LOVE

And we know that in all things God works for the good of those who love him, who have been called according to his purpose. Romans 8:28

I OFTEN THINK ABOUT THE BYGONE DAYS AND HOW AMAZING IT IS THAT GOD BUILT US WITH A FORGIVING SYSTEM. We forget the bad. We forget the pain and the anxieties and the times we took things into our own hands. We forget the squabbles. And when we look back, we remember only the bright, the beautiful, the new, the clear and the pleasant. It's almost a God-given recipe for how we should live daily and what we should hope for. We are made to be positive. We are made with hope. We are made with love and forgiveness. Tonight on New Year's when we look back over the year that's in its last minutes, we know that we were blessed. We know that we are rich in God's love, and we know we need to live like He programmed us.

New Year's always reminds me of puppy dogs—full of hope, bright-eyed and cute, soft and furry, kind and needy, looking for us to care. Puppy dogs and New Year's both make our hearts flutter with excitement.

But the year will turn into a dog.

And it is all up to us how this dog will turn out. Dogs give what they get. They don't ask questions. They are not concerned about tomorrow, and everything you did wrong yesterday is in most cases forgiven before you realize you did wrong. This New Year puppy can be your soul mate for years to come. This New Year puppy can be your protector and give unselfishly all the love that you desire. Puppy love is hope. Hope looking at you. So this year, look at yourself. Consider what you can do to make it good and better. A year from now, God willing, you can honestly say, "I buried the negative vibes, enjoyed the positive, hugged and played, rejoiced and prayed, had a Skipper (the Master of the ship) for my life and trusted that I could turn this puppy into a good dog. One who loves and cares with kind things to share for the New Year to come."

The Pruning of Perspective

He cuts off every branch in me that bears no fruit, while every branch that does bear fruit he prunes so that it will be even more fruitful. John 15:2

THE YEAR STARTED IN A NON-TRADITIONAL FASHION WITH DREARY, GRAY DAYS HERE IN EAST TEXAS. Many days rain poured like there is no end. And so often I get asked, "Is it good for the vineyards?" Time and time again I have to remind myself of the fact that a higher hand controls the things that are not in our control. Most of the time when we don't understand, it is good for us—as long as we do the best with our obligations. In Bullard it was a week full of tragic pain and the shocking realities of mortality that can only be accepted with a perspective of "yesterday is gone and tomorrow is unknown." Those of us who are seasoned, but not salted, reevaluate and live like there is no tomorrow, love like there is no tomorrow and forgive like there was no yesterday.

Nobody gets tired of an "I love you." And nobody knows if the opportunity to hear or say those words will ever be lent again. It's like pruning these vineyards. It doesn't matter if it is cold or rainy or if the sun is shining. If we don't do it when we can do it, the opportunity of time will pass us by and the summer will come. The vineyard will bear fruit from undisciplined vines that will shine through to the last drop of wine. We can blame the rain, and we can blame the cold. But the obligation is on us to do as much as we can when we can. The lessons of this gray beginning are simple and grounded in the laws of nature. But there's nothing worse than self-regret. And there's nothing better than the contentment that I labored, loved and shared the fruits with everyone who needed sharing. Tonight I raise a glass of Cab to all of you who worked today and told somebody, "I love you." Tomorrow somewhere the sun will shine again, and things that seemed so impossible will happen as blessings so undeserved by anyone.

Kiepersol is a food, wine and spirits destination based in East Texas. Estate-grown artisan wines are finely crafted to be comfortable to drink, pairing everyday life with the abundance of the earth. Unique Texas spirits are made on-site to intrigue the most avid connoisseur. Experience a steakhouse dinner, wine and spirits tastings or simply time to recharge in one of our bed & breakfast retreats.

kiepersol.com